AMBER FARIS

The Ulimate Food Guide to Wilmington NC

Discover Where and What to Eat in The Port City

Copyright © 2024 by Amber Faris

All rights reserved. No part of this publication may be reproduced, stored or transmitted in any form or by any means, electronic, mechanical, photocopying, recording, scanning, or otherwise without written permission from the publisher. It is illegal to copy this book, post it to a website, or distribute it by any other means without permission.

Amber Faris asserts the moral right to be identified as the author of this work.

Amber Faris has no responsibility for the persistence or accuracy of URLs for external or third-party Internet Websites referred to in this publication and does not guarantee that any content on such Websites is, or will remain, accurate or appropriate.

Designations used by companies to distinguish their products are often claimed as trademarks. All brand names and product names used in this book and on its cover are trade names, service marks, trademarks and registered trademarks of their respective owners. The publishers and the book are not associated with any product or vendor mentioned in this book. None of the companies referenced within the book have endorsed the book.

First edition

This book was professionally typeset on Reedsy. Find out more at reedsy.com

People who love to eat are always the best people.

Julia Child

Contents

1	Introduction	1
2	Wilmington's Signature Dishes	3
3	Captivating Views	8
4	Coffee Shops and Cafés	16
5	Breakfast and Brunch Spots	24
6	Hidden Gems	28
7	Casual Dining	31
8	Seafood Delights	34
9	International Cuisine	37
10	Fine Dining & Upscale Eateries	40
11	Sweet Treats and Desserts	43
12	Breweries and Bars	46
13	Honorable Mentions	49
14	Conclusion	51
15	References	53
	About the Author	58

1

Introduction

Welcome to "The Ultimate Food Guide to Wilmington," your comprehensive companion to exploring the rich and diverse culinary landscape of Wilmington, North Carolina. Nestled by the Cape Fear River, Wilmington isn't just a picturesque port city with a storied past; it's a vibrant culinary hot-spot that caters to every palate. With over 500 restaurants, around 50 coffee shops, and a burgeoning scene of over 30 food trucks, this city is a hidden gem for food lovers.

    Wilmington's food culture is as layered as its history. From traditional Southern comfort foods to innovative fusion cuisine, the city's culinary scene reflects a unique blend of the old and the new. Tracing back to its roots as a bustling port, Wilmington has always been a melting pot of cultures, evident in its varied gastronomic offerings. Here, you can savor fresh seafood from the Atlantic, indulge in authentic international flavors, or enjoy farm-to-table dishes that showcase local produce.

    In this guide, we'll take you on a journey through Wilmington's best eateries, from quaint brunch spots and family-run diners to high-end restaurants and melt-in-your-mouth desserts. Each chapter is dedicated to a different aspect of Wilmington's food scene, with recommendations, insider tips, and must-try dishes. Whether you're a local foodie or a traveler eager to taste the city's best flavors, this guide is designed to be your ultimate culinary companion.

Embark on this delicious journey with us and discover why Wilmington, NC, is a true paradise for food enthusiasts.

2

Wilmington's Signature Dishes

Wilmington is rich in history and boasts a delectable array of signature dishes that encapsulate the essence of Southern cuisine with a unique coastal twist. Among these culinary delights are my favorites, Hummingbird Cake, She-Crab Soup, Pimento Cheese, and Britt's Donuts. These dishes, each with its own story, collectively represent Wilmington's culinary identity, inviting locals and visitors to indulge in a taste of coastal Carolina charm.

Hummingbird Cake

The South sure knows how to do dessert. While there are many great options, including Key Lime Pie, Banana Bread Pudding, and Coconut Cake, my choice is Hummingbird Cake. The Southern Hummingbird Cake, a delightful and rich dessert, is a testament to the rich culinary traditions of the South. This cake stands out with its moist texture and sweet, fruity flavors. Characterized by its banana bread-like consistency, enhanced with crushed pineapple, it's a unique combination of tropical flavors and down-home comfort. The cake is generously spiced with cinnamon and adorned with chopped pecans or walnuts, adding a nutty depth to its flavor profile. Each layer is filled and frosted with a rich, creamy cheese frosting, offering a tangy counterpoint to the sweetness of the cake.

Where to get it: Sugar Crystals Baking Company 609 Piner Rd.

28412910-398-8998

She-Crab Soup

A staple in Southern coastal cuisine, particularly renowned in Charleston, SC, the She-Crab Soup is a classic, rich, and creamy soup that represents the epitome of comfort in coastal Southern cooking. This luxurious soup is made with heavy cream, a rich seafood stock, and the star ingredient, crab meat from female crabs. The addition of crab roe adds a unique richness and complexity, while a hint of mace or nutmeg contributes a subtle warmth. The soup's velvety blend is typically seasoned and garnished with fresh parsley and a dash of sherry, creating a symphony of flavors.

Where to get it: Oceanic at the Crystal Pier 703 S. Lumina Ave. 28480 910-256-5551

Pimento Cheese

Southern Pimento Cheese, often described as "the caviar of the South," is a quintessential staple in Southern cuisine and can be savored at restaurants all over town. This simple yet indulgent spread combines sharp cheddar cheese, creamy mayonnaise, and sweet pimento peppers, resulting in a creamy, slightly chunky texture. The sharpness of the cheese and the tanginess of the pimentos are balanced by the richness of the mayonnaise, with variations including garlic powder, onion powder, and a dash of cayenne. A symbol of Southern hospitality, pimento cheese at any locale captures the essence of regional culinary traditions.

Where to get it: Ocean Grill & Tiki Bar 1211 Lake Park Blvd S. 28428 910-707-0049

Britt's Famous Homemade Glazed Donuts

Britt's Donuts, a fixture since 1939, is famed for its homemade glazed donuts, consistently making national top 10 lists. These donuts, known for their fluffy texture and sweet glaze, are a testament to the shop's dedication to quality and tradition.

  Each donut is a piece of Wilmington's rich history, offering a simple yet profound culinary experience that embodies the timeless essence of a classic treat. Since its doors opened in 1939, this beloved doughnut shop has become a landmark for locals and sweet-toothed travelers from far and wide.

  The magic of Britt's lies in their uncompromising dedication to quality and tradition. Each donut is crafted with a level of care and expertise that transcends the ordinary. The recipe, honed to perfection over decades, yields donuts that perfectly balance fluffy, airy texture and a sweet, melt-in-your-mouth glaze. This delightful simplicity makes Britt's donuts more than just a treat; they are a culinary experience, evoking nostalgia and a sense of communal joy. Visitors to Britt's are not just buying a donut; they are partaking in a piece of Wilmington's rich history, savoring a tradition that has been sweetening the local food scene for over eight decades. With its enduring popularity and acclaim, Britt's Donuts embodies the essence of what makes a culinary institution legendary.

Where to get it: Britt's Donut Shop 13 Carolina Beach Ave. N 910-707-0755
  Tips: Britt's is only open seasonally and is cash only.

3

Captivating Views

When visiting Wilmington, the allure of its stunning views is an integral part of the experience. This city offers a splendid array of dining options that not only tantalize the palate with delectable fare but also enchant the eyes with spectacular vistas. Whether it's the Atlantic coastline's serene beauty or the majestic Cape Fear River, the scenery complements the culinary delights, creating unforgettable dining experiences.

Oceanic 703 S. Lumina Ave. 28480 910-256-5551

Perched on Wrightsville Beach near the island's south end, Oceanic stands out as a jewel for oceanfront dining. Guests are treated to meals on the Crystal Pier, which extends over the Atlantic Ocean, offering an unmatched view of the water. The restaurant boasts a curated selection of wines and cocktails, perfectly complementing the fresh seafood sourced from local fisheries. For those visiting, complimentary parking in their private lot is convenient, with additional street parking available via pay booths. I recommend beginning your meal with the classic Hushpuppies and the Sun-Kissed Shrimp, drizzled with Thai sweet and spicy chili sauce. For the main course, try the Day Boat Sea Scallop Rigatoni, featuring garlic, white wine, capers, and lemon, or the Lumina Burger, a delightful combination of Applewood bacon, cheddar, lettuce, tomato, onion on a brioche bun with Louie sauce, served alongside Old Bay® fries. Each dish at Oceanic is a celebration of coastal flavors, served in a setting that complements the culinary experience.

Smoke on the Water 3704 Watercraft Ferry Ave. 28412 910-833-5069

Established in 2016 in the Riverlights district, Smoke On The Water is a tranquil haven from the downtown hustle, situated by the picturesque Cape Fear River. This spot is celebrated for its exceptional seafood and its mesmerizing views. Featuring a large firepit, it's the perfect setting for unwinding and immersing in the natural beauty. When it comes to dining, the Fried Brussels Sprouts are a must-try, fried till crispy, tossed in duck fat, topped with smoked bacon and Parmesan cheese, and served with a Green Goddess dipping sauce. Another highlight is the Smoked Prime Rib, a 7oz smoked Prime Rib on toasted French bread, complemented with horseradish cream sauce, grilled onions, and provolone cheese, served with au jus. The Smoked Trio is also highly recommended, consisting of 14-hour smoked brisket in smoked BBQ sauce, pulled Carolina pork BBQ, and smoked chicken wings with a choice of sauce (apple-habanero glazed, roasted peach BBQ, smoked jalapeno buffalo, or raspberry chipotle) accompanied by house-cut French fries and coleslaw. A tip for visitors: Time your visit in the evening to catch a breathtaking sunset that enhances the dining experience at Smoke On The Water.

The George on the Riverwalk 128 S. Water St. 28401 910-763-2052

Located in the bustling heart of downtown Wilmington, The George on the Riverwalk offers a picturesque dining experience along the historic Cape Fear River. This venue is renowned for its Southern Coastal cuisine, presenting a varied menu that includes fresh local seafood, succulent steaks, delightful pasta, tender chicken, and refreshing salads. Additionally, it caters to a diverse range of dietary preferences with vegan and gluten-free options, as well as a dedicated kids' menu. Guests enjoy complimentary off-street parking and can dine in a dog-friendly setting.

For appetizers, you cant go wrong with the George Bacon Chicken Bites with pickled jalapeno, pineapple relish, and romesco sauce, or the Baked Brie with roasted garlic, cranberry chutney, spiced honey raisin, and toasted pita bread. Among the specialties to indulge in is the Grilled 8oz Angus Filet Mignon, served with spinach and garlic mashed potatoes, all drizzled with a white balsamic brown butter. The Fried Dill Pickle Marinated Chicken Breast is another standout, accompanied by Cajun cream gravy, garlic mashed potatoes, and collard greens. Seafood lovers can savor the Black Bass (Barramundi), with coconut rice, spinach, red curry, and pineapple relish. The outdoor seating at The George on the Riverwalk provides stunning views of the Cape Fear Memorial Bridge and The Battleship, making it an ideal location for a memorable dining experience followed by a leisurely stroll along the Riverwalk.

Bluewater Waterfront Grill 4 Marina St. 28480 910-256-8500

Inspired by waterfront living, Bluewater Waterfront Grill at Wrightsville Beach is a local favorite for its casual atmosphere and Carolina hospitality. The menu at Bluewater, deeply rooted in fresh, local favorites, varies with the seasons to showcase the best offerings of North Carolina's fishing season. Perched on the Intracoastal Waterway, diners at Bluewater are treated to stunning panoramic sunset views daily. For added convenience, there's complimentary parking in their private lot, or you can even arrive by boat and dock at the day dock.

When it comes to dining, the Fresh Catch of the Day is a must-try, offering choices like Mahi-Mahi or other fresh catches, perfectly blackened or grilled, served alongside rice and the chef's seasonal vegetables. The Tomahawk is a standout dish for those seeking something heartier, featuring a 10oz pork chop accompanied by pickled cherries, butternut squash purée, collards, and a fennel shallot salad. Other delightful options include the Coconut Shrimp, the indulgent Lobster Mac and Cheese, and the classic Bouillabaisse, each dish capturing the essence of coastal cuisine. Bluewater Waterfront Grill is more than just a restaurant; it's a celebration of the coastal lifestyle, offering an authentic taste of North Carolina.

In Wilmington, the enchantment of dining goes beyond the plate, extending to the breathtaking views that accompany each meal. The restaurants featured in this chapter epitomize Wilmington's unique blend of exquisite culinary artistry and stunning natural beauty. Whether it's the serene embrace of the Atlantic, the tranquil Cape Fear River, or the picturesque Intracoastal Waterway each location offers more than just a meal. They offer an experience that engages all the senses. These establishments are not just places to eat; they are destinations where the scenery is as integral to the experience as the cuisine itself. As you explore Wilmington's dining scene, let these charming views enhance your culinary journey, making each meal a memorable part of your visit to this charming city.

4

Coffee Shops and Cafés

In Wilmington, coffee is not just a beverage; it's a culture. This chapter takes you on a tour of the city's finest coffee shops and cafés, each boasting its own unique brews and specialties. From award-winning lattes to in-house roasted beans, these establishments are the heartbeats of Wilmington's vibrant coffee scene, offering much more than just a caffeine fix.

Maven 3816 Oleander Dr. 28403 910-586-1762

Maven stands out as the premier coffee destination in Wilmington and is widely regarded as the best coffee shop in the city. The Campfire Latte, a crowd favorite, perfectly encapsulates their dedication to unique and high-quality brews. As Nico, the owner, says, "We have the unique blessing to share competition coffees and showcase unique producers. Our goal is to challenge the way people experience and drink coffee." Apart from the popular Campfire Latte, don't miss the Sparkling Piña Matcha and the indulgent Chocolate-Cherry Truffle Latte, each offering a distinct and memorable coffee experience.

COFFEE SHOPS AND CAFÉS

Blue Cup Roastery 348 Hutchison Ln. 28401 910-541-5682

Embodying the motto "Where Habit Meets Happiness," Blue Cup Roastery is a container coffee shop with ample indoor and outdoor seating, making it a perfect spot for both people and their pets. The café prides itself on roasting coffee in-house, ensuring each cup is fresh and full of flavor. Their seasonal menu is always a hit, but the specialty that stands out is The Blue Cup-acino: a unique blend of house-made vanilla syrup and bourbon vanilla marshmallow. "We love seeing our regular visitors and friends with their fur kids, and we look forward to meeting new visitors," shares the owner, Amy H., expressing the warm and welcoming atmosphere that Blue Cup Roastery is known for.

All of these coffee havens in Wilmington offers its unique twist on the classic coffee shop experience. Whether you're looking for a competition-grade latte at Maven or a cozy, pet-friendly environment at Blue Cup Roastery, Wilmington's coffee scene caters to all preferences, be sure to explore these cafés for your daily dose of caffeine and a chance to immerse yourself in the local coffee culture.

Hidden Grounds 21 S. 2nd St. 28401 910-228-5436

Hidden Grounds, a unique backyard oasis coffee bar with a dinosaur theme, offers a whimsical retreat for coffee lovers in Wilmington. This family-owned and operated café, renowned for its pet-friendly atmosphere, invites guests into a world where prehistoric charm meets modern coffee culture. Their most popular offerings include the 'Dino Campfire,' an imaginative latte-style espresso with toasted marshmallow and a torched finish, and the 'Nanner Puddin'', a delightful blend of espresso, banana, caramel, and vanilla, topped with whipped cream and caramel drizzle. The 'Leggo My Eggo' and 'Thai-Rannosaurus Rex' are other standout options for those looking to try something different. Each drink at Hidden Grounds is not just a beverage but an experience, blending creativity with coffee in a truly memorable setting.

COFFEE SHOPS AND CAFÉS

Wilmington, NC boasts a vibrant coffee culture that caters to locals and visitors alike. From charming neighborhood cafes to trendy artisanal coffee shops, this coastal city offers diverse coffee experiences. Whether you are searching for a cozy spot to savor a latte, a bustling cafe for a quick caffeine fix, or a serene location to enjoy a cup of joe, Wilmington's coffee scene has something for everyone. So, the next time you find yourself in Wilmington, explore these delightful coffee shops and cafes to savor the flavors and hospitality that make this city's coffee culture exceptional.

5

Breakfast and Brunch Spots

Start your day in Wilmington with a culinary adventure that will tantalize your taste buds and energize your morning. This chapter of our food guide highlights the top-rated breakfast and brunch spots in Wilmington, each offering a unique twist on morning favorites. From classic Southern comfort to authentic French crepes, these establishments promise a delightful start to your day.

Savor Southern Kitchen 3704 Carolina Beach Rd. 28412 910-769-8112

Renowned for its traditional Southern charm, Savor Southern Kitchen is a must-visit for breakfast enthusiasts. The star of the show is Chef Brad's award-winning Chicken and Waffle – a true Belgian sugar pearl waffle topped with a golden fried chicken breast and candied bacon, all drizzled with Chef's bourbon barrel stout syrup. It's an experience that combines sweetness, savoriness, and a touch of Southern decadence. Other popular dishes include Sweet Potato Biscuits, the Family Tradition Benny, the 'Til The Cows Come Home Bowl, and the famed 'Well Kiss My Shrimp & Grits'.

Our Crepes & More 3810 Oleander Dr. 28403 910-395-0077

For a taste of France in the heart of Wilmington, visit Our Crepes & More. This family-owned-and-operated restaurant, established by French expatriates in 2010, offers an authentic French Crêperie experience. Favorites include the savory Foresticre Royale Crepe, filled with cheese, chicken, bacon, mushrooms, and onions in a creamy sauce, and the sweet St-Tropez Crepe with banana, peach puree, caramel, peaches, and whipped cream. In addition to these, the Tahiti and Quebec savory crepes, as well as the Mont-Blanc and Versailles sweet crepes, are popular choices among patrons. The restaurant also offers the flexibility to build your own crepe with options for Gluten-Free, Dairy-Free, and Vegan batters. Don't forget to try their weekly specialty crepes for something new and exciting.

Brunches 2030 Stonecrop Dr. Ste. 501 28412 910-833-5519

At Brunches, you'll find a delightful mix of classic and inventive breakfast and brunch options that cater to a variety of tastes. This spot is a local favorite for its playful and hearty approach to morning meals. The Chicken Biscuit Supreme remains a crowd-pleaser, featuring open-faced biscuits topped with fried chicken, eggs, and sausage gravy. For those who prefer a twist on the classic, the B.B.O Bronx Bomber – a combination of bacon, ham, sausage, cheese, and eggs – is a must-try.

Other popular items include B.B.O By the Sea, a seafood lover's delight, the classic Shrimp & Grits, and the Notorious BLT, a unique take on the traditional BLT sandwich. The brunch experience at Brunches is further enhanced by their selection of popular brunch cocktails, such as the Bloody Maria, the Twisted Espresso, and the celebratory Birthday Shot. Embodying a fun and relaxed atmosphere, Brunches lives up to its motto, "Mimosas made me do it," offering a perfect setting for a leisurely and enjoyable start to your day in Wilmington.

Tip: Brunches has 3 locations for convenience.

The Kitchen Sink 622 N 4th St. 28401 910-399-4162

The Kitchen Sink offers a cozy, homey setting with a menu that speaks Alicia's love language: food. Start with The Hoop Cheese, a southern-style rosemary biscuit stuffed with eastern NC Hoop Cheddar. Other popular choices include the Lox Eggs Benedict, Harissa Scramble, and B.A.D. Huevos Rancheros. Don't miss the Healing Break Soup – a unique and comforting choice. As Robin says, "We are not fast food. We are elevated."

Tip: The Kitchen Sink isn't just for breakfast; their lunch menu, featuring the popular Beef on Weck, as well as Nonna's Meatball and The Goat, is equally impressive. The restaurant's rotating selection of soups is another highlight, with the option to order a flight for those who want to sample several flavors.

Each of these spots offers a unique glimpse into Wilmington's diverse breakfast and brunch scene, making them ideal destinations for locals and visitors. Whether you're in the mood for a classic Southern breakfast, a French-inspired crepe, or an elevated brunch experience, Wilmington has it all. Remember to check their opening times and consider making reservations where possible, as these popular spots can get busy, especially on weekends. Enjoy your culinary morning in Wilmington!

6

Hidden Gems

Wilmington, a city known for its vibrant culture and scenic beauty, harbors a treasure trove of culinary delights waiting to be discovered. This chapter delves into the heart of Wilmington's food scene to uncover its best-kept secrets. From the innovative twists on classic pretzels at Crofton Pretzels, the nostalgic flavors of Louie's Hot Dogs, and the authentic New York-style pizza at I Love NY Pizza, we explore the hidden gems locals cherish, and visitors yearn to find. These gems are not just places to eat; they are cornerstones of community and tradition, each with a story to tell. Join us on a gastronomic journey through the lesser-known yet equally delightful eateries that make Wilmington a true foodie's paradise.

Crofton Pretzels 1620 Market St. 2840 1 910-236-9667

Nestled in the heart of Wilmington lies a unique culinary delight: Crofton Pretzels. This veteran-owned and operated local business stands out with its specialty in soft pretzels and pretzel-based products. The owner, Aidan, recommends an off-menu marvel - the pimiento cheese-stuffed pretzel dog, a hidden gem for any pretzel enthusiast. This is a brand-new item that Aidan first shared with me for this book!

What sets Crofton's apart is its astonishing variety, boasting a rotating selection of over 20 stuffed pretzel flavors. Patrons can indulge in everything from the savory loaded mashed potato to the unexpectedly delightful dill pickle and even the sweet strawberry cheesecake pretzel. Each pretzel is baked fresh throughout the day, from open to close, right in front of your eyes, adding a touch of performance to the culinary experience.

Louie's Hot Dogs 204 ½ Princess St. 28401 910-763-8040

Since 1989, Louie's Hot Dogs has been a staple of Wilmington's food culture, evoking a sense of nostalgia with every bite. Famous for serving all their dogs on perfectly steamed buns, Louie's offers a journey through flavors and memories.

My favorites are the Babe Ruth, a classic combination of mustard, kraut, and onions; the Latimer, a delightful mix of BBQ sauce, bacon bits, and cheese; and the classic smoked sausage dog. Louie's also boasts other specialties like the Coastline, Courthouse, and the intriguing Scurvy Dog, each offering a unique taste of Wilmington.

I Love NY Pizza Wilmington 28 N. Front St. 28401 910-762-7628

Bringing a slice of New York to Wilmington, I Love NY Pizza is a testament to authenticity and tradition. The founder, Papa Yianni, hailing from a small village in Peloponnese, Greece, opened his first restaurant in 1980. His philosophy of "satisfaction over saving" and treating customers like family is palpable in every slice.

While a simple pepperoni pizza by the slice remains my go-to, the menu extends to whole pizzas, strombolis, and calzones, embodying New York-style pizza's essence. The walk-up window service and late-night hours until 3 AM on Fridays and Saturdays make it a perfect spot for those late-night cravings.

In Wilmington, these hidden gems offer more than just food; they provide a taste of history, tradition, and community. Each establishment's unique flavors and stories contribute to the rich tapestry of Wilmington's culinary landscape. So, savor the flavors of these little-known treasures, whether you're a local or just passing through.

7

Casual Dining

Wilmington's casual dining scene offers a delightful array of choices for those seeking a relaxed atmosphere without compromising on taste. This chapter highlights some of the best spots for casual eats in the city. From mouth-watering burgers to the best southern fried chicken in town, these establishments are perfect for a laid-back meal with friends and family.

Rebellion 15 S. Front St. 28401 910-399-1162

With both indoor and outdoor seating, Rebellion is named in honor of The Whiskey Rebellion, symbolizing a tribute to the struggles and sacrifices of the past. Known for serving what many consider the best burgers in Wilmington, their signature dish is 'The Rebellion' burger – featuring two RBP's, bourbon bacon jam, crispy bacon, aged cheddar, bourbon BBQ sauce, LTO, all on a potato roll. Another must-try is the 'Super Mario's Pork Bites,' fried pork belly with mob rub and charred lime, so delicious you'd want to order multiple servings. Also, don't miss 'The Showboat,' a buttermilk fried chicken sandwich that's a delight in every bite.

Dram Tree Tavern 1806 Washinton St. 28401

This neighborhood bar is all about live music, cold drinks, and tasty food. Dog-friendly with a large fenced area, Dram Tree Tavern offers a chill and casual vibe that's perfect for unwinding. Make sure to try their Taco Tuesday specials – 2 for $5 or 3 for $6.50, which are both delicious and great value for money.

Beat Street 348 Hutchinson Ln. 28401 910-541-5505

Located in The Cargo District, Beat Street is a vibrant, energetic, fast-casual restaurant that's part of the True Blue Restaurant family. Their goal of serving "Vibrant Delicious Authentic Wild Street Food" is evident in their most popular item, the 'SMASH Burger': a 6 oz. bacon grind patty with lettuce, tomato, American cheese, special sauce, and garlic pickles. Chef Kevin, who played a key role in opening all True Blue Restaurants, recommends the newly added Spicy Chicken Bacon Ranch Wrap. Meanwhile, Ruby, a former vegetarian turned meat lover at Beat Street, favors the Chili Crunch Beef Satay.

Rooster & Crow 225 S. Water St. Ste. G & H 28401 910-399-4780

Boasting the title of "Best Southern Food In Wilmington," Rooster and Crow is the go-to place for southern comfort food, especially fried chicken and gravy. Opened in May 2019 by best friend owners, this spot offers a unique experience with its Cryptid Den Bar & Lounge, The Beer Garden, and Fowl Play Arcade. While they offer excellent lunch and brunch options, their dinner steals the show. The Fried Chicken portion is generous, equivalent to half a chicken, served with two sides – ample enough to share and savor.

Although casual dining establishments these will provide excellent food and an atmosphere perfect for relaxing and enjoying good company. Whether you're craving a gourmet burger, a street food delight, or a hearty southern meal, these spots will satisfy your cravings in a laid-back setting. Remember, casual dining in Wilmington is all about enjoying great food in a comfortable, no-rush environment.

8

Seafood Delights

Embark on a coastal culinary journey in Wilmington, where the sea's bounty is transformed into an array of delightful dishes. This chapter in our food guide shines a spotlight on the top seafood restaurants in Wilmington, each bringing a unique flavor to the table. From freshly caught local favorites to innovative seafood fusions, these establishments are set to provide an unforgettable dining experience.

SeaView Crab Company 1515 Marstellar St. 28401 910-769-1554

Immerse yourself in the essence of oceanic flavors at SeaView, a cornerstone of Wilmington's seafood scene. At the heart of their menu is the commitment to freshness, as articulated by Brandon: "We have been providing fresh seafood for the last decade, and it's something we are proud of." Must-try dishes include the Power Bowl, Shrimp Tacos, Battered French Fries, and Fried Okra, each crafted perfectly. Established in 2006 by three seafood-loving friends, SeaView melds tradition with modern culinary techniques, creating a symphony of flavors in every dish.

Michaels Seafood Restaurant 1206 N. Lake Park Blvd. A 28428 910-458-7761

Step into Michaels for a genuine seafood experience with the motto, "Sandy feet welcome - just be ready for real seafood." Established in 1998, this eatery is a treasure trove of culinary delights. Their international award-winning chowder is a testament to their mastery of seafood cuisine. Signature dishes like Bacon Wrapped Scallops, Lump Crab Cake Sandwich, and Seafood Lasagna are not just meals but an adventure for your palate. Michaels offers a warm and welcoming atmosphere with a pet-friendly outdoor shaded patio.

Carolina Crab House 341 College Rd. #55 28403 910-399-6522

Experience the soul of southern seafood at Carolina Crab House. Here, the tradition of enjoying seafood is elevated with a hands-on approach. Choose your seafood, add potato, corn, and egg, and get ready to dive in with your hands, gloves provided. The house sauce, a mix of all other sauces, is a culinary revelation, elevating the simple to the sublime. This dining experience is more than a meal; it's a memorable journey into the heart of southern cuisine.

Fish Bites Seafood Restaurant 6132 Carolina Beach Rd. 28412 910-791-1117

Fishbites is a celebration of seafood innovation, featuring Wilmington's only Live Lobster Tank and a full-service "Bottoms Up Bar." Indulge in their blackened salmon fish tacos, Shrimp & Grits, and other specials like stuffed Flounder or The Fisherman's Stew. Sign up as a VIP for exclusive access to secret menu items and specials. Don't miss their weekly rotating desserts for a sweet finale to your meal.

Bento Box 1121 Military Cutoff Rd. 28405 910-509-0774

For an exquisite fusion of flavors, visit Bento Box, where Chef Lee, Wilmington's Sushi Master, awaits to surprise you with his culinary artistry. This restaurant offers a culmination of Asian street food, with menu options from Japan, Thailand, Vietnam, China, and Korea. The ambiance is as diverse as the menu, featuring a private dining room, an outdoor patio with a zen rock garden, and a sake lounge. Signature dishes like the Dim Sum Sampler, Duck Spring Rolls, and unique sushi rolls such as B.Eel.T., Dynamite, The Hawaiian Crunch, and Komodo Dragon are crafted to feed and enchant.

Wilmington offers a distinct perspective on seafood cuisine, and these restaurants make them essential stops on your culinary voyage. Whether craving a traditional seafood feast or an inventive fusion, Wilmington's seafood scene is a treasure trove. Check their operating hours and consider reservations, as these popular destinations are favorites among locals and visitors. Dive into Wilmington's seafood delights and let the ocean's bounty captivate your senses!

9

International Cuisine

Set off on a gastronomic expedition around the globe without leaving Wilmington. This chapter introduces you to the city's international dining scene, each establishment offering a unique culinary perspective. From authentic Italian fare to the vibrant tastes of Latin America, these restaurants promise a journey through the diverse flavors of the world.

Freddies Restaurant (Italian) 105 K Ave. 28449 910-458-5979

Nestled near Kure Beach pier, Freddies Restaurant, opened in 1995, is a delightful mix of Italian cuisine in an Irish pub ambiance. Famous for its martinis, this establishment is the brainchild of Barbara Gargan, who dreamt of an Italian restaurant specializing in spaghetti and pork chops. Today, it's renowned as the best "pork chop restaurant" in town. Indulge in their house salad, the steak Barb Style adorned with fresh & roasted garlic and mozzarella cheese, and a side of creamy pasta alfredo. Other must-tries include the Chicken Parmigiana and the unique Pork Chops - Peach Pecan or Apple Walnut. Due to its popularity, reservations are advised, though they don't cater to groups larger than 12.

Amanecer Cocina & Cafe (Mexican) 1616 Shipyard Blvd. #20 28412 910-833-5260

Amanecer brings the authentic essence of Mexico to Wilmington. Here, the Fishbowl Mimosa and Mexican Coffee are the talk of the town. The dish to try is the Quesa-Birrias: birria taco quesadillas generously topped with cilantro and onion, accompanied by rice, birria consome, and fresh spicy salsa. Other specials worth sampling are the Enchiladas Verdes, particularly recommended with Birria meat for an enhanced flavor.

Café Chinois (Asian Fusion) 3710 College Rd. #123 28412 910-769-3193

Café Chinois is where French-inspired Asian cuisine meets artistic presentation. Offering a range of dishes from Thai, Vietnamese, Korean, and Chinese traditions, this restaurant embodies the owner's passion for combining food and art. Highlights include Moo Todd, a marinated Thai-style pork deep-fried to crispy perfection and topped with fried garlic, the savory Chicken Satay, Thai Larb Gai featuring ground chicken with roasted rice powder in a spicy lime dressing, and the Vietnamese Bahn Xeo, fresh crepes with shrimp, pork, and bean sprouts, served with lettuce and nuoc cham.

Savorez (Latin Cuisine) 402 Chestnut St. #4026 28401 910-833-8894

Savorez introduces a Latin flair to local Wilmington cuisine, bustling with bold flavors and a welcoming staff. Chef Sam Cahoon's southern spin on Latin dishes results in an array of beautifully crafted, flavor-packed options. Due to its cozy size, the restaurant operates on a first-come, first-serve basis. Begin with the Pineapple Salsa, followed by the LANGOUSTA Y COCO Tapas - lobster ceviche in a citrus coconut ginger marinade with avocado, cilantro, onion, and red bell. The CHORIZO & GOAT CHEESE Empanada with salsa verde and black bean dipping sauce is a must-try, as well as the TRES COCHINITOS - grilled pork loin over black bean-bacon puree, and the CARNE CON ANCHO, an ancho chile rubbed teres major with crispy arepa and a host of delicious accompaniments.

These Wilmington restaurants offer a unique taste of international cuisine, Whether craving the homely comfort of Italian, the vibrant zest of Mexican, the sophisticated fusion of Asian, or the spirited flavors of Latin America, Wilmington's international food scene caters to a myriad of palates.

10

Fine Dining & Upscale Eateries

Regarding fine dining in Wilmington, several high-end restaurants promise a unique culinary experience. From authentic Italian cuisine to innovative American dishes, each establishment offers a unique atmosphere and exquisite dishes, perfect for a memorable evening. Reservations are recommended for these upscale eateries, ensuring you have the ideal table for your special occasion.

Tarantellis 102 S 2nd St. 28401 910-763-3806

Named 2022's "Best Authentic Italian Food In Wilmington," Tarantellis is a family-owned restaurant nestled in the historic district of downtown Wilmington. The owners envisioned creating a warm and comfortable place that feels like home, and they sure succeeded. Inspired by seasonal ingredients, the menu includes authentic Italian dishes made with the finest ingredients. Must-try appetizers include Bruschetta with Wagyu filet mignon and Cavoletti Di Bruxelles Con Pancetta E Burrata. The Pesche Grigliate e Miele salad is a delightful blend of honey-grilled peach and local mixed greens. For pasta lovers, the Fettuccine con Salsiccia e Salvia Fritte is a must, and if available, don't miss the Pumpkin Gnocchi in Brown Butter Sauce.

Manna 123 Princess St. 28401 910-763-5252

Manna offers a fine dining experience that explores the elegance of American cooking. As the proud recipient of the AAA Four Diamond Award every year since 2015, Manna is the only restaurant in Wilmington to have this honor. The menu changes frequently, showcasing the freshest ingredients and providing a variety for regular customers. The chef specializes in French techniques, creating unique combinations and flavor profiles from various cultures. For an exclusive experience, call ahead for their four-course tasting menu. Located in the heart of downtown, Manna also offers exquisitely decorated rental accommodations. If you are coming for a visit definitely check them out.

Caprice Bistro 10 Market St. 28401 910-815-0810

Owned by Chef Thierry Moity and his wife Patricia, Caprice Bistro has been offering a taste of France in Wilmington since 2001. The bistro's authentic and cozy ambiance mirrors that of a quaint Parisian eatery. Start your meal with the Escargots Petits Gris, featuring tender escargot sautéed with garlic in a delectable Roquefort cream sauce, or the Saucisse Lapin, a delightful dish of seared rabbit sausage paired with caramelized onions and jus. For the main course, indulge in the classic Beef Bourguignon, a rich beef stew simmered in red wine with lardons, onions, mushrooms, and carrots, or savor the Duck Confit, crispy duck legs served with artisan lettuce, potatoes, and a flavorful gastrique sauce. Each dish at Caprice Bistro is a reflection of classic French flavors, masterfully prepared with a modern touch.

True Blue Butcher and Table 1125 Military Cutoff Rd. #A 28405 910-679-4473

At True Blue Butcher and Table, Chef Bobby Zimmerman and his team offer cuisine inspired by the best ingredients, curated liquors, beer, and wines. Opened in 2017, True Blue lives up to its name, symbolizing trustworthiness and dedication to quality. The menu features a range of locally sourced ingredients, including 28-day choice and prime beef, local pork and chicken, and imported seafood. For an ideal meal, start with the Green Goddess salad, followed by the Beef and Brussels starter. For the main course, the Pork Belly Ramen and Beef Rib Bolognese are both exceptional choices, making it hard to choose just one.

Whether you're celebrating a special occasion or simply seeking a night of culinary excellence, these restaurants will impress with their sophisticated ambiance, exceptional service, and masterful cuisine. Remember to call ahead for reservations to ensure your fine dining experience is as seamless as it is memorable.

11

Sweet Treats and Desserts

Next we will take a delightful journey into Wilmington's world of sweet indulgences. This chapter is dedicated to those who harbor a love for desserts and seek to explore the best places in the city to satisfy their sweet tooth. From exquisite French pastries to innovative gourmet cupcakes, Wilmington's dessert scene is a paradise for anyone with a penchant for sugary delights.

Far From France 1474 Barclay Pointe Blvd. #201 28412 910-833-5002

Nestled in a charming Parisian bistro setting, Far From France offers a taste of fine French cuisine right in Wilmington. Owners Josephine and Alban Pelletier are committed to providing friendly and efficient service, with a menu that's both deliciously approachable and authentically French. Their LES MACARONS, gluten-free and made with almond flour, are a must-try for anyone seeking a taste of France. Another specialty, LES

MADELEINES, are delightfully light and gluten-free, made with rice flour. Apart from desserts, Far From France also serves lunch, brunch, and dinner. For a unique experience, book a reservation for their French High Tea and immerse yourself in the elegance of French culinary tradition.

The Peppered Cupcake 260 Racine Dr. Ste. 7 28406 910-399-1088

Since its opening in 2008, The Peppered Cupcake has established itself as a true gourmet cupcake shop in Wilmington. With a passion for creating exciting flavor combinations, this cupcakery turns the concept of a regular cupcake on its head. "The Peppered Cupcake is a gourmet cupcakery." says the owner. The motto, "Not just a dessert, it's an experience," truly encapsulates what they offer. The cupcakes, adorned with true buttercream, feature ingredients like fresh fruit, warm compotes, fresh pepper jellies, homemade caramel and ganache, whipped creams, and toasted nuts. With a rotating selection of flavors, there's always something new and exciting to try. Favorites include the Blueberry & Lavender, Spicy Maple Bacon, and the unique Lemon Curry.

The Jelly Cabinet 1011 N. 4th St. 28401 910-745-0327

The Jelly Cabinet, a delightful new addition to Wilmington's culinary landscape since July 2023, is quickly becoming beloved among locals and visitors alike. With a focus on scratch-made pastries and confections, this charming establishment is known for its irresistibly delicious Cinnamon Rolls. The menu boasts other irresistible treats, such as Blueberry Biscuits,

Matcha Coffee Cake, Dulce de Leche Brownies, and the unique Biscoff Cinnamon Bun. Each bakery item is a testament to their commitment to quality and flavor. A tip for those planning to visit: The Jelly Cabinet is open exclusively on Saturdays and Sundays from 8 AM to 2 PM, making it a perfect weekend destination for indulging in sweet, homemade delights. Their emergence on the scene promises longevity, adding a special touch to Wilmington's vibrant food culture.

Wilmington offers a unique experience for dessert havens, be it a trip to a Parisian bistro at Far From France or a culinary adventure with The Peppered Cupcake. Whether you crave the classic elegance of French pastries or the bold, innovative flavors of gourmet cupcakes, Wilmington's dessert scene promises to enchant and satisfy. Explore these sweet destinations for an unforgettable end to your meals or as a delightful treat any time of the day!

12

Breweries and Bars

Wilmington's brewery and bar scene is as rich and diverse as its history. This chapter invites you on a journey through some of the best local breweries and bars, each offering a unique take on craft beers and cocktails. From solar-powered brewing processes to 1920s speakeasy vibes, Wilmington's establishments are not just about drinks; they're about experiences.

Mad Mole Brewing 6309 Boathouse Rd. Unit C 28403 910-859-8115

Dubbed "Mad About Beer," Mad Mole Brewing combines the owners' names and a playful nod to the "mad scientist" concept, reflecting the scientific precision they bring to brewing. This brewery, operating on a seven-barrel electric system, is distinctively powered by solar energy, aligning with its mole theme to create beer "brewed by the sun." At Mad Mole, you can indulge in a variety of Belgians, IPAs, and more, each carefully crafted with a passion for beer and science. Located near Wrightsville Beach in Wilmington, Mad Mole is a must-visit for craft beer enthusiasts. The Cupcake Citra Mole Down comes highly recommended.

End of Days Distillery 1815 Castle St. 28403 910-399-1133

End of Days Distillery embraces the philosophy that what's in your glass is more than a drink; it's a celebration of life. The distillery offers guided tours that explore the intricacies of sourcing, fermentation, distillation, and finishing. Visitors get to savor the distinct flavors of their heritage spirits, including exceptional gin, vodka, and rum, each expressing the unique character of Carolina roots. Gin lovers should try the Luna Bloom Butterfly Pea Flower Gin. The Lounge at End of Days is the perfect spot to enjoy hand-crafted cocktails like The Ruby, Violet Sunset, or Yaupon Sour.

Edward Teach Brewery 6604 N. 4th St. 28401 910-523-5401

Named after the infamous pirate Blackbeard, Edward Teach Brewery brings a pirate theme to life. Since its opening on December 15, 2017, it has offered a selection of 8 draft beers. "We wanted something that was indigenous, and lent itself well to the region," says owner Gary Sholar. The Teaches Peaches Peach Ale is a standout, a light-bodied ale with peach and apricot puree, offering a slightly tart finish. The downstairs bar, resembling the front of a pirate ship like the "Queen Anne's Revenge," provides an immersive pirate experience.

The Blind Elephant 21 N. Front St. 28401 910-833-7175

This speakeasy, inspired by the classic 1920s, is a craft cocktail and bourbon bar that has recently celebrated its 10-year anniversary. Tucked away in an abandoned alley in downtown Wilmington, The Blind Elephant operates with a $5 member entry fee. Known for its selection of whiskeys, bourbons, rye, and exceptional cocktails, it also offers live music regularly. Each cocktail, including their impressive mocktails, is unique and expertly crafted, providing a delightful experience to visitors.

If you want a unique glimpse into the local beverage culture, these breweries and bars are ideal destinations for locals and visitors. Whether you're in the mood for a craft beer brewed with scientific precision, a heritage spirit distilled with care, a pirate-themed ale, or a classic cocktail in a speakeasy setting, Wilmington has it all. Dive into these establishments to taste local brews and spirits, and immerse yourself in the rich flavors and stories they offer.

13

Honorable Mentions

Numerous eateries deserve a special mention in Wilmington's vibrant and diverse dining landscape. These establishments, each with their own unique flair and culinary offerings, contribute significantly to the city's rich gastronomic tapestry. From artisanal sandwiches to authentic international cuisines, these honorable mentions are must-visit spots for those looking to explore the full spectrum of Wilmington's food scene.

1. **CheeseSmith** - Celebrated for its artisanal cheese-based dishes.
2. **New Day Cafe** - A welcoming café known for its fresh and inventive menu.
3. **Mess Hall** - Offers creative and satisfying culinary delights.
4. **Salita Pizza** - A favorite in Wilmington for its delicious pizzas.
5. **Zocalo** - Distinguished for its vibrant atmosphere and authentic cuisine.
6. **Henry's** - A classic spot for hearty American comfort food.
7. **Indochine** - Renowned for its original and flavorful Asian

dishes.
8. **Nori** - A go-to for fresh, innovative sushi and Japanese cuisine.
9. **Jay's Incredible Pizza** - Known for its outstanding pizza creations.
10. **Ann Bonny's Bar and Grill** - Ideal for relaxed dining and enjoyable drinks.
11. **Kilwins** - Famous for its delectable desserts and sweet treats.
12. **The Vault** - Offers a unique and creative dining experience.
13. **Ibis Coffee and Cocktails** - Known for its exquisite coffee blends and sophisticated cocktails.
14. **BullCity Cider Works** - A hub for unique and refreshing cider varieties.
15. **Szechuan 132 Chinese Restaurant** - A top choice for authentic Szechuan flavors.

Each of these venues contributes to the rich tapestry of Wilmington's dining scene, offering experiences that range from casual bites to gourmet feasts. Whether you're seeking a quick coffee, a cozy meal, or an elegant dinner, these honorable mentions are perfect for any occasion, reflecting the city's diverse and vibrant culinary identity.

14

Conclusion

As we conclude our culinary journey through "The Ultimate Food Guide to Wilmington," it's evident that this charming port city is a treasure trove of gastronomic delights. Wilmington's food scene is a vibrant tapestry woven with threads of tradition, innovation, and a deep love for quality and flavor. From the humble yet iconic Britt's Donuts to the sophisticated offerings of high-end eateries, each chapter of this guide has revealed a facet of Wilmington's culinary identity. The city's ability to harmonize its rich history with contemporary tastes sets it apart as a food lover's paradise.

The diversity of the dining experiences in Wilmington – be it the comforting embrace of Southern classics, the fresh bounty of the sea, the exotic flavors of international cuisine, or the inventive allure of food trucks – ensures that there is something to satisfy every palate and occasion. The coffee shops and dessert spots add a sweet note to the city's culinary symphony. At the same time, local breweries and bars offer a spirited glimpse into Wilmington's artisanal craft scene.

In Wilmington, every meal is more than just sustenance; it's an opportunity to connect with the city's culture, people, and history. As you explore the streets of this coastal gem, let your taste buds lead the way. Whether you're a resident rediscovering your city or a visitor experiencing it for the first time, Wilmington's culinary landscape is a continuously unfolding story, inviting you to be a part of its delicious narrative.

So, take this guide as your starting point and create flavorful memories. With each bite and sip, you're not just tasting food; you're experiencing the heart and soul of Wilmington. Bon appétit!

15

References

Carolina Beach | Federal Point | Britts Donut Shop. (n.d.). Britts. https://www.brittsdonutshop.com/

Home - True Blue Butcher & table — We are true blue. (n.d.). We Are True Blue. https://www.wearetrueblue.com/truebluebutcherandtable

Crepes | Our Crepes & more. . . | United States. (n.d.). Ocm2015. https://www.ourcrepesandmore.com/

Your seven day a week brunch destination specializing in mimosas and other brunch cocktails. (n.d.). Brunches. https://www.mimosasmademedoit.com/

Home - Bluewater Waterfront grill. (2023, November 14). Bluewater Waterfront Grill. https://www.bluewaterdining.com/

Smoke on the water. (n.d.). Smoke on the Water. https://smok

eonthewater.squarespace.com/

The Kitchen Sink. (2023, July 4). *Fresh food in Wilmington NC - The Kitchen Sink Restaurant.* https://thekitchensinkilm.com/

The George on the riverwalk. (n.d.). https://thegeorgerestaurant.com/

CAROLINA CRAB HOUSE. (n.d.). https://carolinacrabhouse.com/#

Restaurant, M. S. (n.d.). *Michael's Seafood Restaurant.* Michael's Seafood Restaurant. https://mikescfood.com/

Kitchen & Deli. (n.d.). Seaview Crab Co. Online Store. https://www.seaviewcrabcompany.com/pages/kitchen-deli

Louie's Hot Dogs | Wilmington NC. (n.d.). Facebook. https://www.facebook.com/louieshotdogs/

CROFTON'S PRETZELS. (n.d.). CROFTON'S PRETZELS. https://www.croftonspretzels.com/

Rooster and the Crow. (n.d.). *Rooster and the Crow.* Rooster and the Crow | the Best Southern Food in Wilmington, NC. https://www.roosterandthecrow.com/

Beat Street. (n.d.). Beat Street. https://www.beatstreetilm.com/

Dram Tree Tavern | Wilmington NC. (n.d.). Facebook. https://w

REFERENCES

ww.facebook.com/dramtreetavern/

Home | Rebellion NC. (n.d.). Rebellion NC. https://rebellionnc.com/

Home - True Blue Butcher & table —We are true blue. (n.d.). We Are True Blue. https://www.wearetrueblue.com/truebluebutcherandtable

Wilmington, NC Restaurant | Home | Caprice Bistro. (n.d.). Caprice Bistro. https://www.capricebistro.com/

housermedia. (2022, March 9). *manna | A Culinary Experience | Wilmington, NC.* Manna Avenue. https://mannaavenue.com/

The Jelly Cabinet | Wilmington NC. (n.d.). Facebook. https://www.facebook.com/p/The-Jelly-Cabinet-100093125971072/

Tarantellis. (n.d.). Tarantellis. https://www.tarantellis.com/

Blind Elephant Speakeasy Historic Wilmington North Carolina. (n.d.). Blind Elephant Speakeasy Historic Wilmington North Carolina. http://www.blindelephantspeakeasy.com/

Edward Teach Brewery – Wilmington NC. (n.d.). https://edwardteachbrewery.com/

EOD Distillery - Wilmington, NC. (n.d.). EOD Distillery - Wilmington, NC. https://www.eoddistillery.com/

Mad mole Brewing – mad about beer. (n.d.). https://madmoleb

rewing.com/

The Jelly Cabinet. (n.d.). Bakery in Wilmington. https://the-jelly-cabinet.business.site/?utm_source=gmb&utm_medium=referral

Amanecer Cocina & Café 1616 Shipyard Boulevard - Order pickup and delivery. (n.d.). Storefront. https://order.online/store/amanecer-cocina-&-caf%C3%A9-wilmington-25081472/?hideModal=true&pickup=true

Admin_Savorez_R. (n.d.). Home. Savorez Restaurant. https://savorez.com/

Asian Fusion Restaurant | Café Chinois | Wilmington, NC. (n.d.). Café Chinois. https://www.cafe-chinois.com/

Freddies Famous Italian Restaurant Kure Beach, NC – A Pleasure Island favorite, since 1994. (n.d.). https://freddiesitalianrestaurant.com/

Bento box. (n.d.). Bento Box. https://www.bentoboxsushi.com/

Fish Bites Seafood Restaurant - restaurant in Wilmington, NC. (n.d.). Fish Bites Seafood Restaurant. https://www.fishbitesseafood.com/

Best Cupcakes | ThePepperedCupcake | Wilmington. (n.d.). ThePepperedCupcake. https://www.thepepperedcupcake.com/

REFERENCES

Far from France menus. (n.d.). https://farfromfrance.com/menus/

About the Author

Amber Faris, is a dedicated foodie and enthusiastic kayaker, with a profound love for reading.

Made in the USA
Middletown, DE
07 April 2024

52527292R00038